The Number One

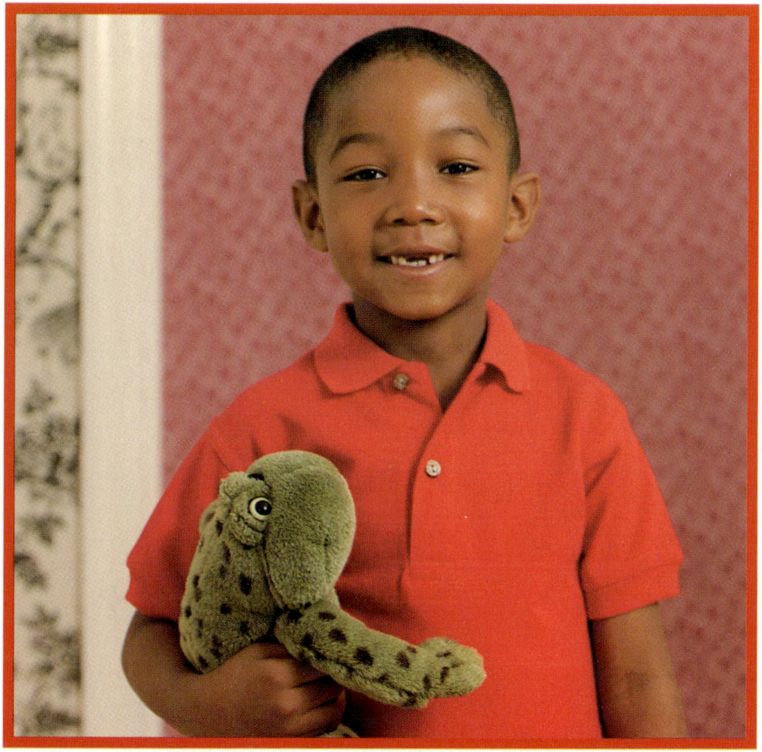

Adria Klein

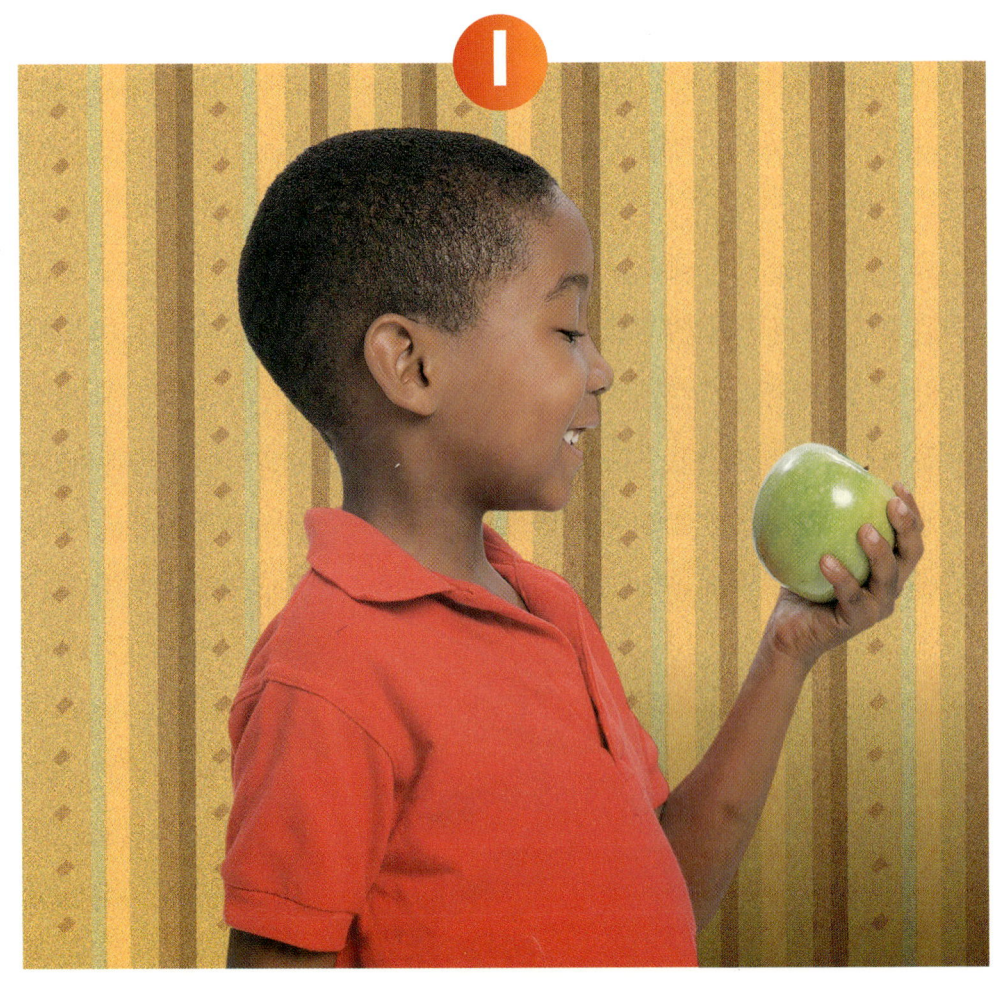

Dashawn wants one apple.

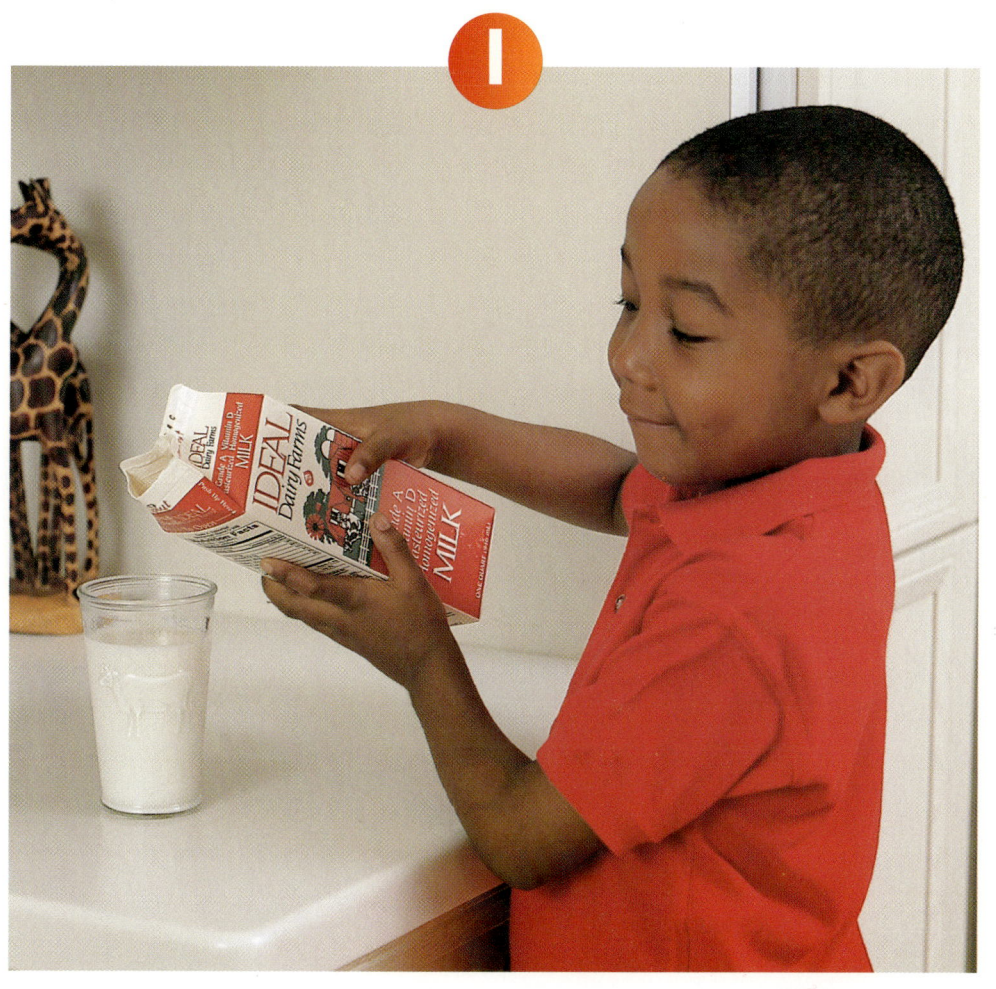

He wants one glass of milk.

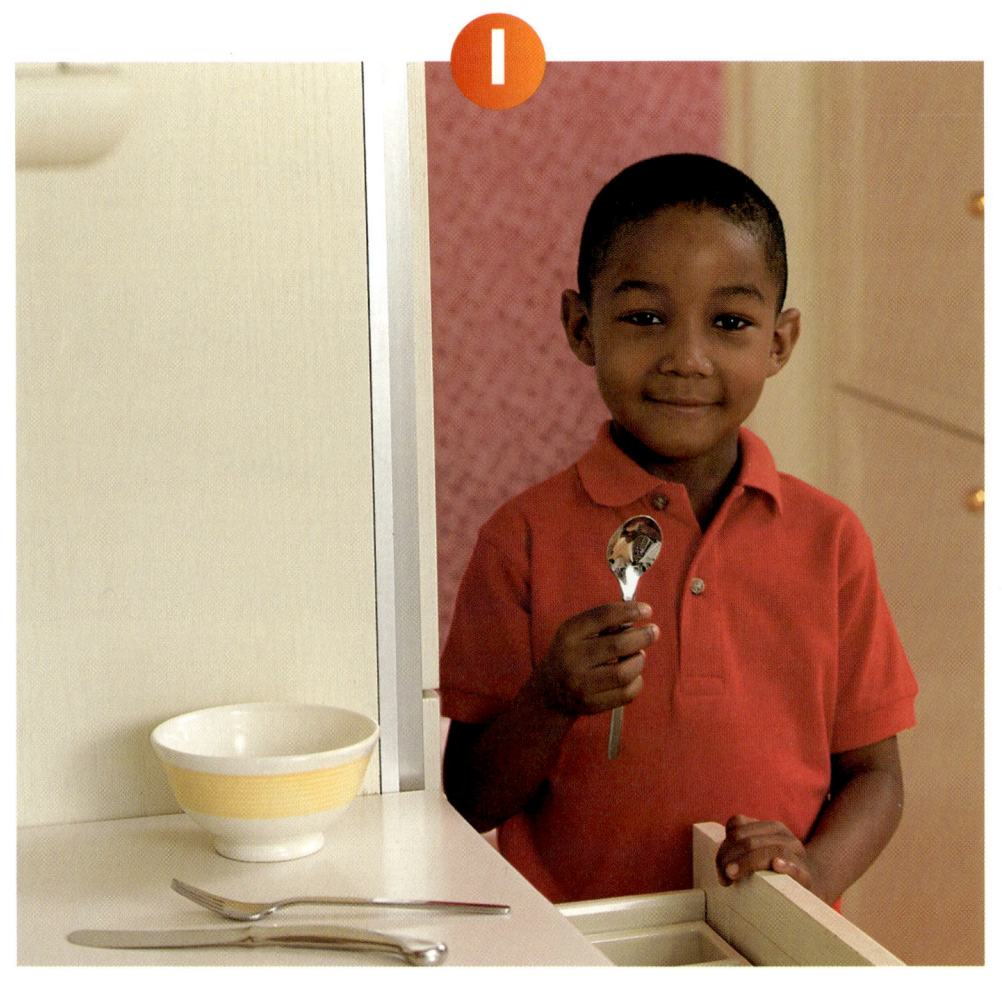

He wants one spoon.

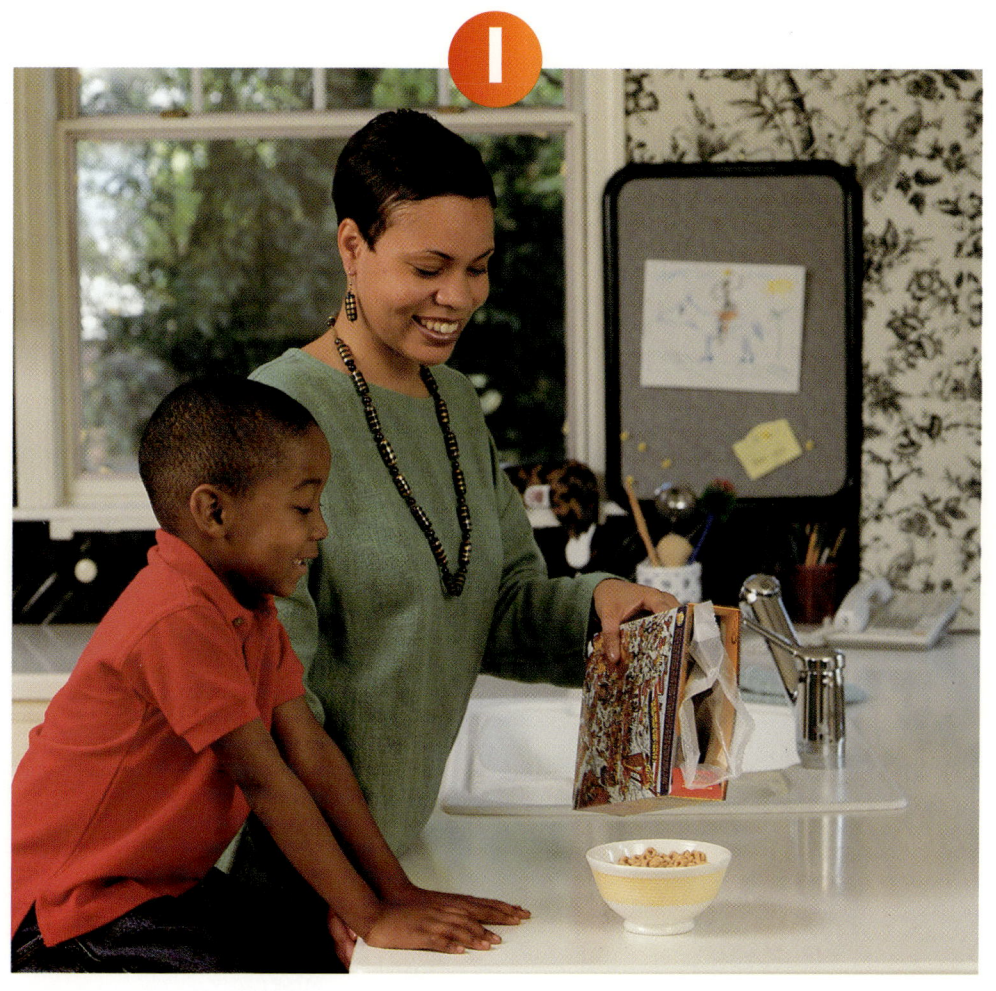

He wants one bowl of cereal.

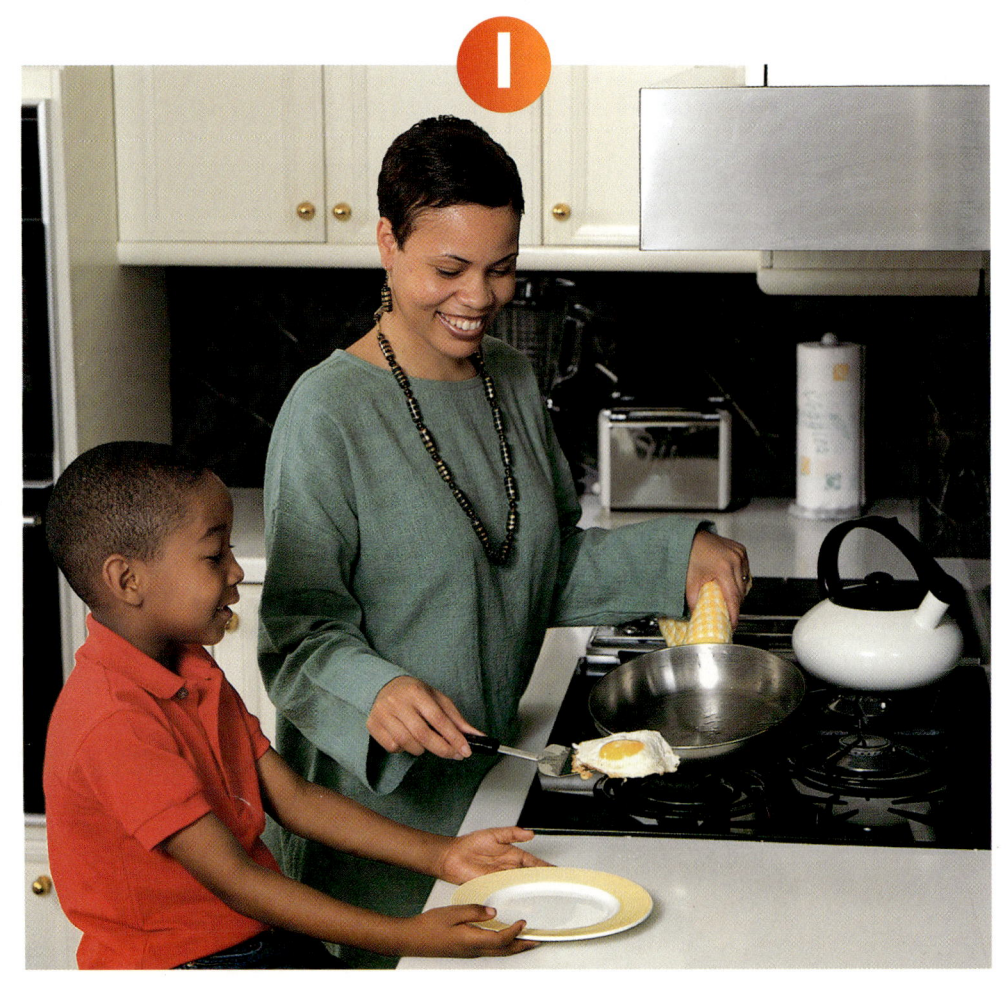

He wants one egg.

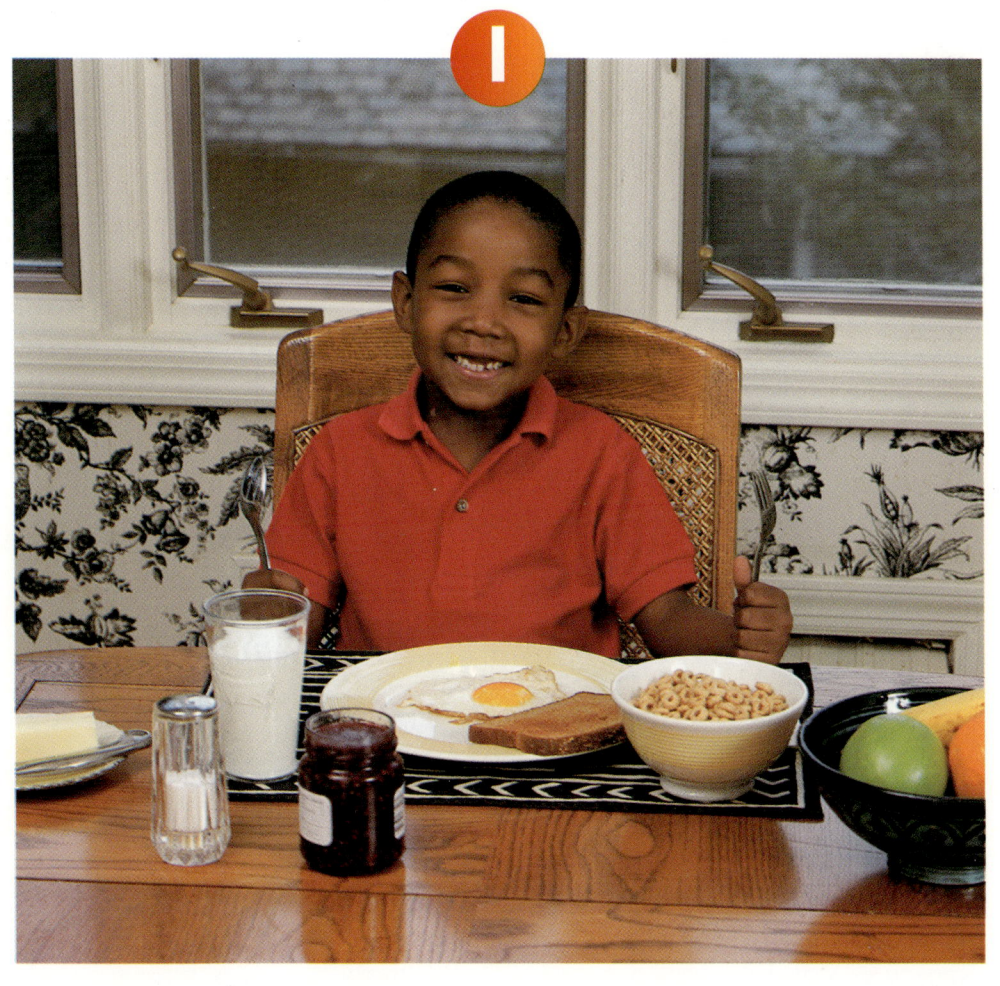

Dashawn wants one big breakfast!

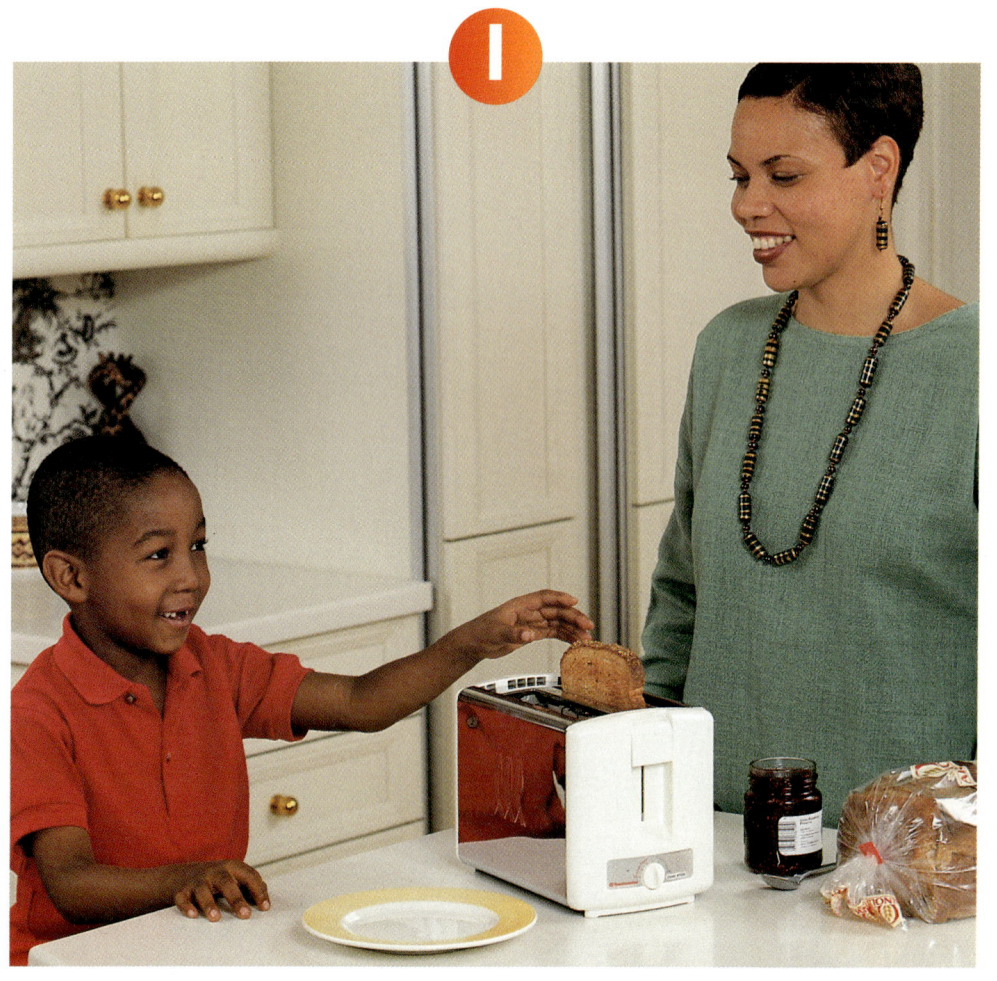

He wants one piece of toast.